HOME SERIES

HOME SERIES
KITCHENS

BETA-PLUS

CONTENTS

P. 4-5
A kitchen by Wilfra in a project by interior architect Philip Simoen.
Table and chairs in grey leather (Zanotta) from Loft Living. The kitchen wall is in marble mosaic from Dominique Desimpel. Wooden floor in untreated walnut wood.

P. 6
Groep Moris designs and creates kitchens in a sober, authentic style. Furniture in aged oak and kitchen surface in white Carrara marble.
A La Cornue range cooker.

FOREWORD

T he kitchen has undergone a metamorphosis in recent years, becoming a new living space.

This phenomenon is closely related to our modern way of life and a growing interest in the culinary arts and design.

Kitchens of the new generation take pride of place in the home, often forcing the dining room or living room to surrender a few square metres.

Symbolising both hospitality and lifestyle, the kitchen often serves a number of purposes: it is a practical space that is both aesthetically pleasing and multifunctional.

The boundaries between the different spaces in the home are blurring and disappearing. This development is a reflection of modern affluence and our more open attitude to the pleasures of life.

As the perfect space in which to come together and share stories, the kitchen has become a reception room for friends and family.

The keyword in these reports is personality. Every kitchen is unique and reflects the owners' way of life.

P. 8
A symphony of white shades in this kitchen by artist Mariette Teugels: Italian marble on the floor, white Delft wall tiles and a white La Cornue range cooker.

P. 10-11
A project by Stephanie Laporte (The Office).
The kitchen unit is in dark oak veneer with concealed handles and an Emperador stone surface. White Lotis lighting. Floor in Cotto d'Este.

AN INTERPLAY OF LINES

AND PERSPECTIVES
IN A MULTIFUNCTIONAL SPACE

T his report features elegant minimalism in a high-tech designer kitchen.

Architect Van Ravestyn has successfully adapted a 1960s kitchen to conform to our modern-day living standards without disturbing the authentic architecture and volumes.

In order to improve the circulation within the house, the architect abandoned a traditional division into separate spaces and removed the walls to create a uni-que, unstructured space in which the garden is an important additional factor.

The dining room, kitchen, living room and library now form one coherent and functional space.

P. 12-15
An intelligent combination of functionality and aesthetics: the architect has created a practical kitchen and dining area that is also the perfect space for entertaining guests. The warmth of the dark wood contrasts with the cool stone.
The colour of the stainless-steel fittings harmonises with the rest of the kitchen. A Viking cooker.

TIMELESS INSPIRATION

A classic kitchen in painted
wood with a bluestone work
surface.

A lthough he also designs complete interiors, designer Benoît Bary's greatest passion is planning kitchens in a timeless style.

Just like every individual, each kitchen has its own personality: "Every home, and, even more so, every kitchen, must reflect the character of the owners, not that of the designer," says Benoît Bary.

These photographs of three of his kitchen designs are striking illustrations of this personalised approach.

A stylish, classic kitchen with a cosy atmosphere. A Smeg cooker, bluestone work surfaces, handles in brushed metal and white Delft wall tiles.

P. 18-19
One of Benoît Bary's first projects: units with bowed doors beside an Aga stove, a baroque design and classic tiles in this nostalgic kitchen.

RESPECT FOR MATERIALS

AND TRADITION

T he family company Tack has been designing and creating kitchens for three generations.

Each of Tack's projects reflects the company's respect for materials and traditional craftsmanship.

Every kitchen is unique, but Tack's kitchens all clearly demonstrate the importance of perfect symmetry and proportion.

The work surface is in aged bluestone with a contoured edge.
Obvious symmetry around the large Lacanche cooker: a display cabinet on either side of the extractor hood. The Art Nouveau cornice is identical to the extractor surround.

The bench, a Tack design, was painted to harmonise with the shades in the kitchen, the chairs and the custom-made table.
Tack also coordinated the colours and lighting.

This unit contains a side-by-side fridge and freezer combination.

Symmetry is also the keyword in this kitchen with a Lacanche range cooker.
Work surfaces and walls in Jura stone. Fitted furniture in hand-painted oak.

P. 24-25
This kitchen, created in a restored castle, is a little
different from the usual kitchens that we expect to
find in such prestigious buildings.
A successful and original interpretation in trendy
taupe and orange shades. A Lacanche stainless-
steel cooker and a wall in Moroccan zeliges. The
floor is in reclaimed bluestone tiles. Table in old oak
and, on the left in the background, an old butcher's
block. The open fireplace also serves as a grill.

THE AUTHENTIC KITCHEN

OF A PROVENÇAL MAS

T his Provençal *mas* was built on the site of a seventeenth-century Carmelite monastery.

The current residents restored the historic house and its beautiful kitchen with the help of May and Axel Vervoordt, respecting the authenticity and traditional atmosphere of the property. The antique building materials helped to preserve the flavour of the kitchen.

P. 26 and 28-29
The kitchen and dining area with a Viking cooker. The old sinks are original features of the building.

This dressmaker's table is from a local second-hand furniture dealer.

Reclaimed terracotta tommettes on the floor.

A SUBTLE MIX OF CONTRASTS

Fahrenheit is not only a renowned designer of kitchens, but also a distributor of range cookers and exclusive kitchen accessories.

The four projects in this report show the great care and attention that the company devotes to each of its kitchens, with an emphasis on durability, high-quality materials and a perfect finish.

The owners of this large villa dating from the 1950s had the brilliant idea of transforming one of their two garages into a large, contemporary kitchen where the whole family could come together. Fahrenheit created a professional kitchen in this new room. The solid oak planks harmonise with the Azul Cascais natural stone. The cooking island consists of a Lacanche cooker with a very large oven.
This dramatic extractor is a custom-built piece in stainless steel and glass, built to original designs by Fahrenheit's Thierry Goffin.

The wall separating this space from the second garage is clad in solid oak planks and incorporates storage space and the door to the garage. The open fireplace is large enough to use as another cooking area.

P. 32-33
A challenging task in a small apartment: creating a new, well-equipped kitchen in the middle of the living area, so that the original kitchen could be given a new function. The result is convincing: a modern, elegant and streamlined room.
Dark oak for the island and MDF for the wall units, painted in the same colour as the walls.
The entire false ceiling functions as an extractor. Kitchen work surface in carefully selected white Carrara marble.

A sophisticated and chic atmosphere in this small, chocolate-coloured kitchen in painted MDF, in a contemporary duplex apartment. The kitchen is part of a large living area with a concert piano, oversized sofas and a plasma screen.
Work surfaces in taupe-coloured stone from Charles Kreglinger. The wall lamps add to the library-like appeal of this space.

A spectacular look for this distinctive, luxurious kitchen in a sumptuous and elegant home. The owners, who are from London, wanted to create a dramatic effect through the almost exclusive use of black. The furniture, the Viking cooker, the work surfaces and the zeliges are all in gleaming black. The only exceptions are the sandstone floor and the stainless-steel fridge.

18th-CENTURY INSPIRATION

Architect Bernard De Clerck created this monumental kitchen in a country house for a family with three young children.

He designed the house in a classic, eighteenth-century style, taking his inspiration for the design of this unique project from a bishop's house dating from 1750.

Left, the kitchen with a view of the dining room and living room. The floor is in a combination of limestone and bluestone.
The chimney above the Aga range is in decorative plasterwork. In the background (photo above), a view of the back entrance, with oak panelling.

The sinks and work surface are in dark-red porphyry. A view of the morning terrace and the courtyard.

The washing room beside the kitchen. Furniture finished in apple-green paint.

CLEAN LINES AND SIMPLICITY

I n his search for manufacturers who shared his design philosophy, industrial designer Ivo de Groot came across the Italian company Strato.

These reports demonstrate how a true symbiosis of unique design and a quality finish can deliver outstanding results.

Strato's techniques and materials were a perfect match for these ultramodern designs.

The front panels in this Strato kitchen are in sandblasted oak veneer.

The Strato concept in action in this kitchen/dining room.

This ultramodern designer kitchen was created in close collaboration with architect Dao Le-Nhu. Front panels in grey stratocolor. The stainless-steel work surfaces have a satin finish. Side panels also in stratocolor.

ANNO DOMINI 1642

A rchitect Bernard De Clerck restored this house dating from 1642, transforming it into a contemporary home for a family with three children.

The owners wanted to make optimal use of all of the rooms by incorporating the beautiful surroundings, natural light and high-quality stone, wood and plaster-work.

The kitchen has a country atmosphere, with a feeling of calm and simplicity, in perfect harmony with the landscape around this country house.

P. 46 and above
De Clerck exposed the original vaulted ceiling of the kitchen. The old
fireplace accommodates bluestone units and a modern cooker by Delaubrac.
Wall in Moroccan zeliges. The island is in bleached oak.
The designer retained the original floor and used it as the basis for the
colour palette in this kitchen.

A view of the dining area, as
seen from the kitchen.

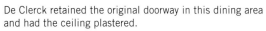

De Clerck retained the original doorway in this dining area and had the ceiling plastered.

The glass doors open up completely, giving this space the feeling of a covered terrace. Floor in old bricks.

Walls in rough wooden planks; floor in bluestone.

Built-in kitchen furniture with old doors. Reclaimed taps.

A whitewashed finish for the walls of the wine cellar.

An old bluestone sink on brick supports. Walls with a whitewashed finish.

A SURPRISING MARRIAGE

OF COPPER AND NATURAL STONE

A n extravagant cocktail of copper and natural stone, designed by architect Wim Goes and created by Top Mouton. Van Den Weghe supplied and installed the stone.

A striking contrast and an unusual combination of two materials (white Calacatta marble and Belgian bluestone) produce a fascinating and remarkable result.

P. 52-55
A harmony of Belgian bluestone (on the floor), Calacatta stone (for the walls) and copper (for the fitted furniture).

IN SEARCH OF DAYS GONE BY

F rancis Van Damme is a master in reclaiming old, lived-in objects and materials and bringing them back to life, creating a rural ambience in warm and cosy kitchens.

Van Damme's traditional workshop has an atmosphere of days gone by: old apothecary's store cupboards, complete nineteenth-century grocery shops, panelling from grand houses and historic manors. Van Damme combines all of these elements to create wonderfully distinctive furniture and decoration for 21st-century clients.

This kitchen was designed in a wasted space in a country house in Normandy. The kitchen unit with bluestone surface is beautifully integrated into this historic house.

Aesthetic and functional aspects combine in this kitchen built around a Lacanche cooker.

P. 58-59
Francis Van Damme found all of the furniture for this kitchen. His staff then painstakingly restored the pieces and installed the kitchen.

A new life for some display cabinets from a London school.

This cupboard came from the same school in London.

A SCENT OF NEW ENGLAND

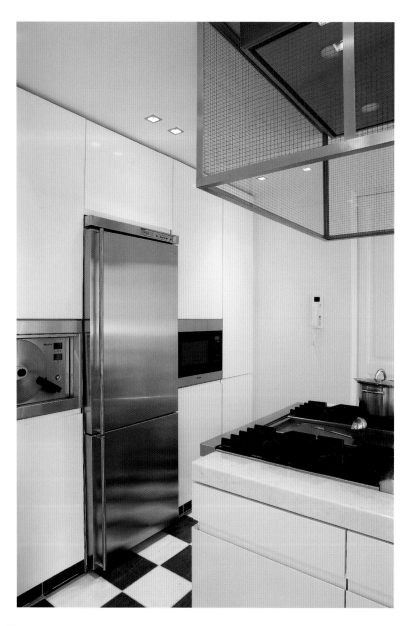

I nterior architect Esther Gutmer was commissioned to create a New England ambience in this holiday home.

The contrast between the dark wood of the floor and the light wood in the kitchen ensures a light and airy atmosphere with a summer holiday feeling.

A view through the sliding doors of the study, which are fully integrated into the walls. The parquet floors throughout the home are in dark mahogany.

P. 64-65
The breakfast room in a bow window.

THE SOUL OF THE HOME

B rigitte and Alain Garnier, a married couple who are both antiques dealers, feel that the kitchen is the true soul of the home.

This kitchen in their former home is a striking illustration of Brigitte Garnier's home-design philosophy: "My ideal home is an old country house with a family atmosphere all day long, sophisticated, with warm colours, a garden that is always green and with lots of space. The kitchen is at its centre, because I love inviting people round and cooking an informal dinner in a large and welcoming kitchen."

An inviting atmosphere in the Garniers' kitchen, around an Aga cooker. The furniture was built from 18th-century panelling, using traditional methods.

ECCENTRIC AND ECLECTIC

The kitchenette is completely
integrated within the wall units.
Wall and work surface both in grey
mosaic.

T he client in this project, which involved furnishing a loft, is a flamboyant French antiques dealer and art collector, with eccentric and eclectic tastes.

As a basis, interior architect Stephanie Laporte opted for a sober contemporary look, decorated with a sumptuous mix of antiques, art and unusual pieces.

The dining room is in a classic wallpaper design in shades of purple with a matching carpet. The concrete structure is visible here. In the background, a collection of antique consoles. The stairs to the dining room are in grey mosaic.

VERY BRITISH IN STYLE

B ritish designer Clive Christian has gained worldwide renown for the perfect finish of his kitchens, bedrooms, bathrooms, dressing rooms and studies.

These kitchen designs beautifully illustrate Clive Christian's selling points: traditional craftsmanship, luxury, an eye for detail and a timeless, classic look.

In this report, the Amazing Interiors consultancy demonstrates how well the British style of Clive Christian travels to other countries.

P. 74-75
Period elements, but in a contemporary context: kitchens by Clive Christian, as seen by Amazing Interiors, are functional and have an atmosphere that is both inviting and timeless.

A SYMPHONY

OF BLACK AND WHITE

T his *bel-étage* home in the city centre has been thoroughly restored to create a home where you can enjoy a glass of wine on your own or party with friends.

Stephanie Laporte has altered the circulation through the building, fashioning an elegant and minimalist living space.

In the foreground, the sitting area with furniture by Mies van der Rohe.

The kitchen unit (with Knoll barstools designed by Bertoia) functions as a link between kitchen and dining room. The large stainless-steel cooker is an eye-catching feature in this kitchen.

THE HEART OF THE HOME

C hef and *traiteur* Christian Souvereyns believes that the kitchen is most definitely the heart of the home: it is an open room where people can cook and eat and chat, where the children can do their homework and play, and where the whole family can come together.

Cooking is an important part of Souvereyns' daily ritual, as his kitchen shows.

A sink area in bluestone and Moroccan zeliges. On the floor, old terracotta tiles.

P. 80-81
The cast-iron Aga cooker occupies pride of place in this kitchen.

STYLISH AND SERENE

Designer Bert Quadvlieg is well known for his restorations of hotels, castles and old farmhouses in Provence and on the Côte d'Azur and many private homes throughout Europe.

His greatest passion is the kitchen. Quadvlieg has designed countless kitchen projects in a wide variety of styles over a period of ten years.

This report features one of his creations: the metamorphosis of a small space to create a large kitchen and adjoining dining room in a house in the style of the Den Bosch School.

Opposite and 84-85
The original terrazzo floor was retained and is a beautiful match for the zinc-fronted units with their oak frames. The work surface is in bluestone.

The oak table and the wrought-iron lamp are Quadvlieg designs.
The chairs are Italian, dating from the second half of the eighteenth
century, and are upholstered in anthracite-grey linen.

INSPIRED BY THE PAST,

ANCHORED IN THE PRESENT

F lamant Home Interiors is a Belgian company that has rapidly gained a strong reputation within the field of interior design, both at home and internationally.

The Flamant style is inspired by the past: reproducing old furniture and reintroducing antique decorative elements that are transformed into distinctive lamps, coffee tables, and kitchen furniture.

This style is inspired by many influences from elegant interiors: beautiful country houses in western Europe, southern England, Scandinavia, Long Island, and also the colonial style.

Vermont model, painted in Tennis White (Original Paint Collection by Flamant). A Cornuchef Grand Papa cooker by La Cornue (130cm). The work surface (3cm thick) is in Belgian bluestone.

Vancouver model in natural oak. Work surface (6cm thick) in bluestone.

Saint-Louis model, painted in Bords de Seine. Work surface in bluestone (3cm thick).

A Long Island kitchen, painted in Grey Pepper.

Vancouver model in natural oak.

Flamant Original Paint Collection. Work surface in honed
Carrara marble (6cm thick). A Smeg cooker, a steam oven and
a Miele coffee machine.

A VAULTED FARMHOUSE KITCHEN

Architect Bernard De Clerck restored this farmhouse, dating from the early nineteenth century, recreating the authentic atmosphere of days gone by.

The architect's vision can clearly be seen in the photographs of the kitchen in this historic farmhouse.

The design is reminiscent of the vaulted cellar kitchens of that era and shows the architect's respect for historic heritage and the craftsmanship of previous generations.

This timeless project is also a modern-day interpretation of our rich architectural history.

On the floor, a mixture of grey and beige French stone tiles. The walls are finished in a pigmented plaster technique.

P. 93-95
The sink is in Luberon stone. A Lacanche cooker and greige zeliges.

A HARMONY

OF BURGUNDY AND BLACK

T his colourful kitchen shows the passion of kitchen desi- gner De Menagerie for streamlined forms, attention to detail and a relentless quest for perfection.

This concept is both functional and aesthetic and was developed in harmony with the space.

P. 98-100
A harmony of black (the Aga cooker and the Moroccan zeliges) and the burgundy of the walls and extractor chimney. The work surface and the island are clad with a 5cm-thick slab of Massangis stone with a contoured edge. The double sink is also in Massangis stone. Kitchen furniture in solid, patinated oak. Taps by Perrin & Rowe. Oak baseboard.

The fireplace wall and dining area were created in collaboration with architect Bart De Beule. MDF shelves for books and wine, with an oak-look finish.

TRADITIONAL KNOW-HOW

O ver the years, Hatabel has created dozens of complete interiors, but the company has made its reputation mainly for the design and construction of custom-built kitchens using time-honoured methods.

Whether the project is a country kitchen or a contemporary one, all Hatabel kitchens are the result of skill and craftsmanship, used to create a lively and inviting atmosphere.

This kitchen was custom-built in hand-painted MDF on the basis of a design by the architect and the client.
Work surfaces and floor in honed bluestone. Sinks in stainless steel; wine rack and blinds in beech.

This kitchen in hand-painted MDF was tailored to the client's requirements. Work surfaces in Rustenburg granite and a porcelain sink.

This third creation by Hatabel was designed in a more contemporary style, with streamlined forms. Kitchen in veneer with built-in lighting in the glass wall.

105

ARCHITECTURAL KITCHENS

T his report presents three kitchen projects by De Menagerie.

Whether it's a rustic kitchen or a kitchen in a modern style, De Menagerie always finds the essence of each project, giving all of its designs a warm and timeless atmosphere.

For every new project, De Menagerie develops a concept in harmony with the space, where functionality and aesthetics go hand in hand.

All of the kitchens are tailor-made and every design is unique, but always made with the same high standards of quality and long-lasting, exclusive materials.

A pleasant mixture of function and comfort. A Viking cooker and an American Amana fridge in harmony with natural wood. The wall behind the cooker is in Moroccan zeliges.

P. 108-111
This kitchen was designed around the majestic stainless-steel La Cornue cooker. Kitchen furniture in solid oak. Work surfaces and sink in bluestone. The dining table, the bench and the shelves are also in oak.

The impressive professional Viking cooker is the eye-catching feature of this kitchen, built in solid American walnut wood. Work surfaces in bluestone.

A VERY COLOURFUL KITCHEN

nterior architect Axel Pairon took his inspiration for this seaside apartment from the modernity of saturated colours.

The house has a very informal ambience and visitors feel the holiday atmosphere as soon as they step through the door.

Derek Wilson designed this kitchen. The large work of art is by Marleen Kunnen: this formed the source of inspiration for the lively palette of colours throughout the apartment.

A COSMOPOLITAN APPROACH

E nsemble & Associés: an appropriate name for a team of two female interior architects who work together. All of their projects are characterised by streamlined design, with light and an eye for detail as key features.

Every project by Ensemble & Associés is carried out in close collaboration with the client. This kitchen in an apartment of over 300m2 is a fine illustration of their approach.

P. 116-119
Bulthaup produced the ultramodern kitchen in this light and airy apartment. Floor in Cotto d'Este and work surface in grey composite stone.
The parquet floor is in grey tinted oak with a matte varnish. In the background of the photograph on the left, the Knoll chairs and large table (320 x 150 cm) are custom-made pieces in tinted oak and gleaming chrome.

HOME SERIES

Volume 2 : KITCHENS

The reports in this book are selected from the Beta-Plus collection of home-design books: www.betaplus.com
They have been compiled in a special series by Le Figaro in French language: Ma Déco

Copyright © 2009 Beta-Plus Publishing / Le Figaro
Originally published in French language

PUBLISHER
Beta-Plus Publishing
Termuninck 3
B – 7850 Enghien
Belgium
www.betaplus.com
info@betaplus.com

PHOTOGRAPHY
Jo Pauwels

DESIGN
Polydem - Nathalie Binart

TRANSLATIONS
Laura Watkinson

ISBN: 9789089440334

Printed in China

P. 122-123
A streamlined contemporary kitchen designed by interior architect Filip Van Bever. Basaltina lava stone has been used throughout this project, for the floors, work surfaces and walls. Stone by Van Den Weghe.

P. 124-125
The kitchen of a farmhouse restored by Virginie and Odile Dejaegere. The aged bluestone (tiles, work surfaces, sinks) is combined with reclaimed terracotta tommettes.

P. 126-127
A project by architect Stéphane Boens. Floors in old terracotta tiles, work surfaces in red marble.